PROJECTS FOR
CHRISTMAS

14

16

18

20

Mary Ann Gree

Illustrated by Janos Mar

WINTER FESTIVALS

The winter solstice, on 21 December, is the shortest day of the year. For thousands of years, people have held festivals on this day, as they looked forward to the return of the sun after the long dark days of winter. One celebration which took place in ancient times was a fire festival, known as the Birthday of the Unconquered Sun.

The Romans and the Norsemen also celebrated the winter solstice by lighting fires. The fire symbolized the light and warmth which the sun provides. The Roman Saturnalia was a wild, unruly festival which began on 17 December. It was closely followed by the January Kalends, when the Romans celebrated the New Year. Houses were decorated with evergreens, gifts were exchanged and masters changed places with their servants. This was supposed to show that all people were equally important.

The ancient Norsemen lit fires in honour of their god Thor, at a festival called the Feast of Juul. Their customs gradually mingled with those of the Celts and spread through many parts of Europe. Many of these Celtic traditions survive today.

As more and more people became Christians, the pagan festivals were renamed and given Christian meaning. The early Christians began to celebrate the birth of Christ at the time of the old winter solstice. When we celebrate Christmas today, we are taking part in a festival which has existed for centuries.

Above *Schools often put on nativity plays, which tell the story of Jesus's birth.*

Left *Trying to guess what is in the parcels is part of the fun of Christmas.*

People celebrate Christmas in different ways. Schools often put on nativity plays and carol concerts. Many Christians go to church late on Christmas Eve. Services sometimes start with the church in darkness; as midnight approaches, candles are lit to celebrate Christ's birth.

For many people, however, Christmas is simply a time for enjoying themselves with families and friends. Exchanging cards and presents has become a part of Christmas. These pictures are fun to paint and can be made into cards to send to your friends.

THUMBPRINTS

You will need:
- **paper**
- **a piece of kitchen sponge on a saucer**
- **poster paint or ink**
- **coloured pens**

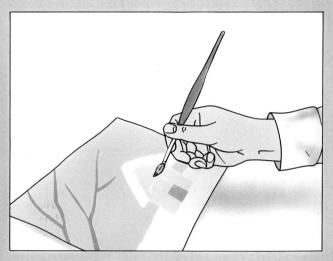

1 Paint a snow scene. Try not to fill the picture up too much — you need to leave room for your thumbprints.

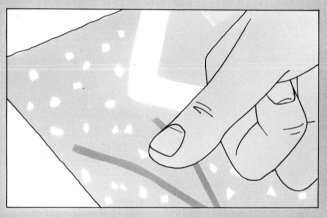

2 When the paint is dry, mix more poster paint. Pour on to the sponge to make a printing pad.

3 Make a thumbprint on your paper. When dry, use your pens to add a beak, wings and a tail and make a robin.

4 Experiment. Try adding different legs, horns and beaks to make other animals and birds.

ADVENT CALENDARS

The period which includes the four Sundays before Christmas is known as Advent and it is the time when Christians prepare to celebrate the birth of Christ. It is followed by Christmas Eve.

In Germany Advent is widely celebrated, with Advent candles and wreaths decorating most of the homes. The Advent wreath is made from interwoven fir twigs and is bound with bright red ribbon. It has four candles. The first is lit on the first Sunday in Advent. One more is lit on each of the following Sundays, until all four burn together.

No one really knows when Advent wreaths were first made in Germany but it is thought that they were brought over from Sweden. They are similar to the Nordic 'Crown of Lights'.

The twenty-four days before Christmas can be counted on the Advent calendar which starts on 1 December. Some calendars have twenty-four windows to be opened, one for each day of Advent. You can make this German calendar for your home or classroom. It is in the form of a wreath and has twenty-four little boxes, each one containing a small gift. If you do not have enough boxes, you can wrap the gifts in strong wrapping paper instead.

Right *Any evergreens can be used for the wreath. Holly looks pretty but may be difficult to work with.*

MAKING A CALENDAR

You will need:
- **thick wire or cane (2 lengths of 100 cm)**
- **sticky tape**
- **sprays of evergreen leaves**
- **scissors**
- **button thread**
- **4 m red ribbon (2.5 cm wide)**
- **24 small toys or wrapped sweets**
- **24 matchboxes**
- **coloured wrapping paper (plain or striped looks best)**
- **12 m red ribbon (5 mm wide)**
- **adhesive gold numbers 1–24**

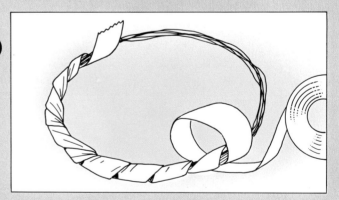

1 Make both lengths of wire or cane into a circle 30 cm in diameter. Bind together with sticky tape.

2 Cut the evergreens into 15 cm lengths. Bind them on to the frame using button thread to hold them in place. Lay the sprays in one direction and overlap each group of leaves a little as you work round the circle.

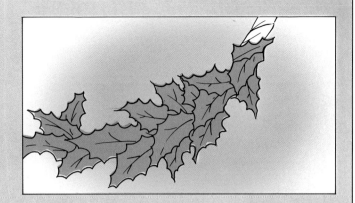

3 Cut the wide ribbon into four equal lengths. Spacing them evenly, tie one end of each ribbon securely to the wreath and gather the four free ends together to make a knot. If you can hang the wreath up now it will be easier to work on.

4 Put a small toy, or two or three wrapped sweets, in each matchbox and make it into a parcel. Leave one end of the wrapping paper free and tie round with narrow ribbon. Leave enough ribbon to attach the parcel to the wreath.

5 Number all the parcels 1–24 using the adhesive stickers.

6 Tie the parcels all round the wreath so that they hang at different heights. Any ribbon left over can be made into a bow to decorate the hanging knot.

CHRISTMAS LANTERNS

At one time the burning of candles in home and church to celebrate Christmas was banned. Church leaders thought candles were pagan symbols, like the fires which were lit to celebrate the winter solstice.

Eventually, however, candles became an established part of the Christmas celebrations. According to tradition, a candle in the window lit the way to Bethlehem for the Holy Family. The lighted candle also symbolizes Christ, who is known as 'the Light of the World'. Now, for all religions, the lighted candle represents the continuance of hope and faith.

Christmas in New York City. Light is still an important part of modern celebrations.

OPEN LANTERN

You can make these lanterns from thick metal craft foil. If this is difficult to find, use large frozen food containers. The pattern is pricked out with a knitting needle.

You will need:
- **heavyweight gold foil**
- **compasses and a ruler**
- **scissors**
- **greaseproof paper**
- **a polystyrene tile**
- **glue and sticky tape**
- **2 knitting needles (one large, one fine)**
- **a metal lid 8 cm in diameter**
- **a night-light**

Safety note
Always use a night-light in your lanterns, as it will extinguish itself if tipped over.

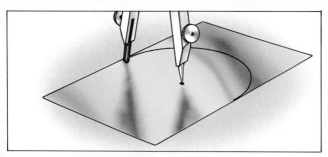

1 Cut a rectangle of foil 17 × 25 cm and mark the centre. Using your compasses draw a semicircle 17 cm in diameter on the top half of the rectangle.

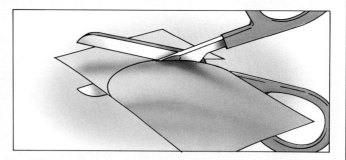

2 Cut along the line of the semicircle. The offcut will make the front of the lantern. Mark the centre at the top and bottom of the large section.

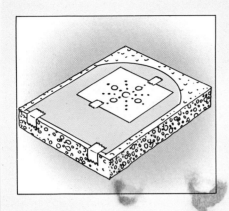 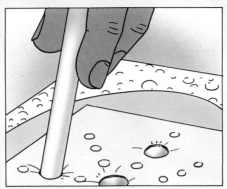 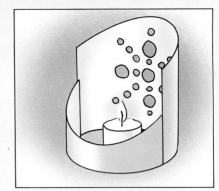

3 Draw a pattern of dots on to a 10 × 10 cm piece of greaseproof paper. Lay the foil on top of the tile. Secure the drawing over the foil 2.5cm from the top edge, with the centre of the drawing over the centre of the foil.

4 Using both knitting needles, punch out the pattern through both paper and foil, taking care that the holes do not overlap.

5 Using the offcut as the front section, join the front and back sections with glue. Tuck the side edges of the front into the back. Stand a night-light in the tin lid and place the lantern over the top.

PAPER-BAG LANTERN

In New Mexico these are called *farolitos* and at festival time can be seen in their hundreds, lining the streets and sitting on adobe walls guarding the rooftops. For safety reasons, use these lanterns outside.

You will need:
● **a heavyweight brown paper bag at least 24 cm wide.**
● **coloured pens (optional)**
● **dry sand or fine gravel**
● **a night-light**

Draw a design on the paper bag with coloured pens. Place the bag on a dry surface and fill with sand to a depth of 7 cm. Place a night-light in the sand. Turn the top of the bag over to keep rigid and light the candle.

PAPER HATS AND CROWNS

In some European countries the Christmas celebrations begin on St Lucia's Day, 13 December. St Lucia was martyred for her Christian beliefs. She came from Sicily, where her day is still celebrated with a fire festival.

In Sweden she is known as the patron saint of light. Each town has its own Lucia queen, who walks from house to house at dawn, wearing a long white dress and a crown of bilberry twigs and candles. She is accompanied by her white-clad attendants, the girls with tinsel in their hair, the boys all wearing tall paper cones covered in stars.

Each family also has its own celebration. It is usually the youngest girl in the family who wakes her parents at first light with a breakfast of coffee and saffron-coloured Lucia buns.

Above *St Lucia's Day celebrations are held in several European countries. This procession is in Sweden.*

ST LUCIA CROWN

You can make this crown for a St Lucia queen and a tinsel headband for each one of the queen's attendants.

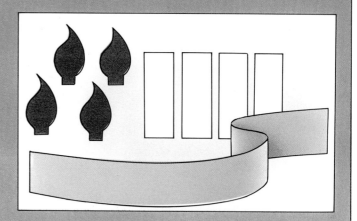

You will need:
- **thin gold card**
- **thin white card**
- **scraps of red metallic card**
- **glue and scissors**

1 Cut a strip of gold card 6 cm deep and long enough to go round the head with a 2.5 cm overlap. Cut four rectangles of white card 12 × 4 cm. Cut four red flame shapes with a flat tab at one end.

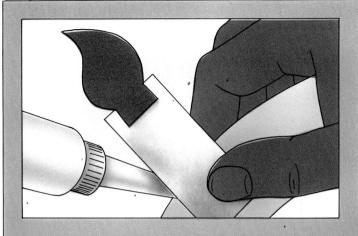

2 Glue the flames to the rectangles to make the candles. Glue the four candles to the inside of the headband, spacing them equally apart.

3 Close the headband to fit and glue or staple to secure. If added decoration is needed, staple little sprigs of evergreen round the gold band.

STAR BOY'S HAT

You will need:
- **a sheet of white/sugar paper**
- **scissors, staples and glue**
- **gold and silver paper or adhesive stars**
- **fine hat elastic**

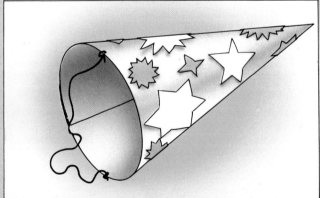

1 Draw a circle (big enough to fit around the head) on the paper and cut out. Mark the centre of the circle. Make a cut from the outer edge to the centre and fold it into a cone shape. Staple to secure.

2 Cut out stars of different sizes from the gold and silver paper. Glue them all over the hat. Cut a piece of elastic to fit under the chin and tie a knot at each end. Staple this to each side of the hat at the lower edge.

Left *Spiced biscuits can be made in all sorts of shapes and sizes.*

For centuries baking spiced cakes and biscuits has been part of the Christmas tradition. They are often flavoured with ginger, which was introduced to Europe by the Romans, who brought it over from their African colonies.

The biscuits are sometimes made in the shape of oxen and pigs. Another traditional shape is the wreath, which represents the completed year. It has a hole in the centre to take a candle.

In Holland and Germany, in particular, special wooden biscuit moulds are used for shaping the biscuits into intricate designs. The dough is pressed into the floured mould, then turned out on to a baking sheet and cooked in the usual way.

SPECULAAS

These Dutch biscuits can be made a week or two before Christmas and kept fresh in an airtight tin. On Christmas Eve, thread them with ribbon and hang them on the tree.

Safety note:
Remember to use oven gloves when removing the biscuits from the oven.

You will need:
- 150 g plain flour
- ¼ level tsp baking powder
- a pinch of salt
- 75 g butter
- 75 g Barbados sugar
- 1½ level tsps mixed spice
- 50 g flaked almonds
- 1 egg yolk
- 1–2 tbsps milk
- biscuit cutters 6 cm in diameter in various shapes
- narrow red ribbon

1 Sift the flour, salt and baking powder into a mixing bowl and rub in the butter.

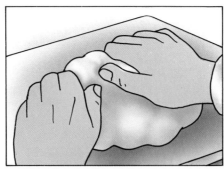

2 Stir in the sugar, spice and almonds. Add the egg yolk and a little milk. Knead to a soft dough.

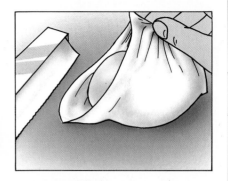

3 Wrap the dough in a piece of foil and leave it to rest for at least an hour in a cool place.

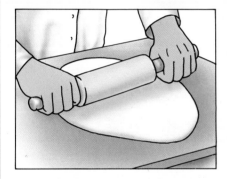

4 Grease one or two baking sheets. Dust the working surface with flour and roll out the dough to a thickness of 5 mm.

5 Cut out the shapes. Before baking, make a small hole through the top of each biscuit using a skewer. Bake for 15–20 minutes at 175°C; Gas 4.

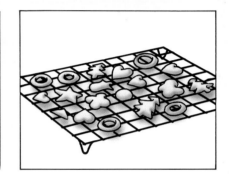

6 Cool the biscuits on a wire tray. You can add extra decoration with piped royal icing. Store until needed.

7 Thread the biscuits with red ribbon and hang them on the tree.

You might like to draw your own shapes for the biscuits. If so, draw the shapes on to card and cut out to make a template. If the shapes are to be bigger than 8 cm in diameter, roll out the dough a little thicker.

CHRISTMAS CARDS

Many people send cards at Christmas. The very first Christmas card was produced in 1843. Early cards were just decorated visiting cards, but as the custom of collecting them became more popular, the designs became more elaborate.

The robin with his red breast featured in many of the designs. Traditionally, he was thought to have brought fire to the earth and so was considered lucky. In the past, postmen wore red jackets and were known as the 'Robin Postmen'.

STAND-UP CARD

You will need:
- **thin card and scissors**
- **coloured pens or poster paints**

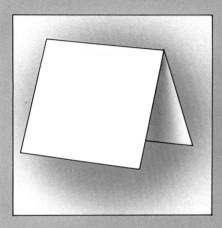

1 Cut out a rectangle of card and fold it in half.

2 Open the card out flat. Draw and decorate a snowman. Make sure his head and shoulders come just above the fold line.

3 Cut round the head and shoulders only. Fold the top section back so that the head stands up above the fold.

3-D CHRISTMAS TREE

You will need:
- **thin card**
- **scissors**
- **sequins**
- **glitter**
- **glue**

1 Cut out two rectangles of card and fold them in half. Draw the outline of a Christmas tree on the top card. Make sure the fold line runs through the centre of the tree shape. Cut out through both pieces of folded card.

2 Open out and decorate both sides of the two tree shapes with glitter and sequins. Keep clear of the folded line.

3 Cut a slit down the fold line of the first tree to within 6 cm of the base. Cut a 6 cm slit upwards from the base of the second tree.

4 Slot the shapes together and open the card out.

CRACKER CARD

You will need:
- **stiff paper**
- **coloured pens**
- **a ruler**
- **scissors**

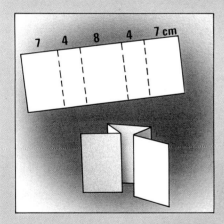

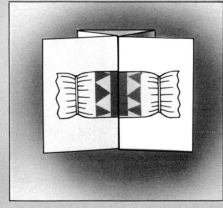

1 Cut a rectangle of paper 30 cm × 10 cm. Measure and mark the points along the edge of the rectangle for the fold lines. Fold as shown.

2 Using your coloured pens, draw a Christmas cracker on the front of the folded card.

3 Open the card and continue drawing across the centre section. Draw jagged edges in the middle as if the cracker has been pulled. Write a message in the centre.

FEEDING THE BIRDS

Danish farmers spread hay on the frozen ground for the deer to feed on at the start of the Christmas season. They also hang out the traditional *juleneg*, a sheaf of oats, to provide food for the birds. Apart from being a sacrifice to the fertility gods, the *juleneg* was thought to be a magic means of protecting next year's crops from the birds. The Norsemen brought this custom to England and in many places garlands of corn are hung on farmhouse doors at Christmas.

WREATH FOR THE BIRDS

You will need:
- **thick galvanized wire**
- **wire cutters or heavy duty scissors**
- **raffia**
- **hay for padding**
- **a bunch of mixed corn – oats, barley, wheat**
- **a darning needle and button thread**
- **whole peanuts, dried fruit, dates, suet, bacon rinds**

If you hang this wreath in a sheltered spot near a window, you can watch the garden birds feeding.

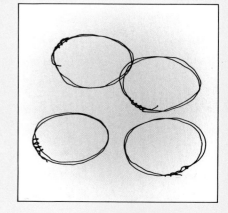

1 Cut the wire into four lengths of 100 cm. Make each length into a circle 30 cm in diameter. Bind together with raffia.

2 Pad the wire thickly with hay and secure with tightly bound raffia. Mark the top and bottom centres with a coloured thread.

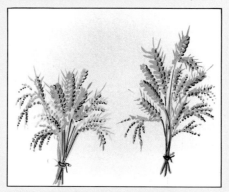

3 Trim the stalks of the corn to about 12 cm and group in little bunches.

4 Starting at the top left-hand side and working downwards, stitch the bunches of corn to the hay base. Attach them in groups of three, laying them at alternate angles as if making a plait.

5 Complete the right-hand side in the same way. Remove coloured thread.

6 Thread the nuts and dried fruit on to lengths of cotton and intertwine them among the bunches of corn. Hang pieces of suet at the bottom. You can add bacon rinds, too, if you have any. Thread a loop of raffia at the top for hanging.

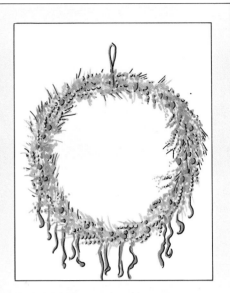

POPCORN GARLANDS

Decorating the Christmas tree with strings of popcorn has become a tradition in Canada and the USA. When Christmas is over, they can be hung outside for the birds.

You will need:
● **butter**
● **a saucepan with lid**
● **unpopped corn (maize)**
● **salt**
● **a needle and strong thread**

Safety note:
Be very careful when using the cooker. Ask an adult to help you.

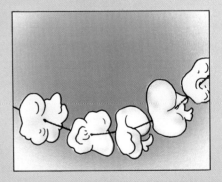

1 Melt a knob of butter in the saucepan. Put a single layer of corn in the saucepan and add a pinch of salt. Do not overfill the pan, as corn expands as it cooks.

2 Put the lid on the pan and keep shaking it every now and again to keep the corn moving. After a while you will hear the corn begin to pop.

3 When all the corn has popped remove the pan from the heat. Turn the corn on to a plate. Thread it on to lengths of cotton and drape them round the Christmas tree.

STARS

Stars have become the universal symbols of Christmas. They are supposed to reveal the presence of God. It was the star over Bethlehem that told of Jesus's birth.

Some people believe that the Pole Star, in the north, is the centre of the universe and it has become a symbol of the Gate of Heaven. It features in Hindu marriage rites as a symbol of constancy.

According to some legends, you should not light the candles on your Christmas tree until the first star becomes visible on Christmas Eve.

Although they can be cut from paper and card, stars for the tree look better made from foil so that they reflect the colours of the fairy lights.

STAR OF DAVID

This six-pointed star is often used to commemorate Chanukah, the Jewish Festival of Lights.

You will need:
- **double-sided craft foil**
- **a protractor**
- **a ruler and pencil**
- **scissors**

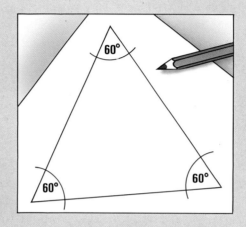

1 Using your protractor, draw an equilateral triangle on to the foil. Make the sides 30 cm in length. The angles at the corners should be 60°.

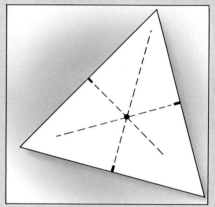

2 Mark the centre of each side and from these points find the centre of the triangle. Cut it out.

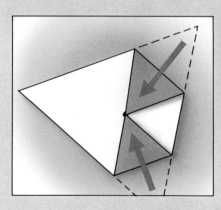

3 Fold all three points of the triangle into the centre, making a hexagon.

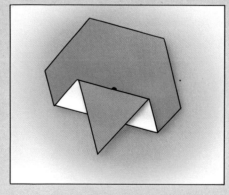

4 Turn over and fold each of the three sections again, taking the outer edges to the centre and turning out the points.

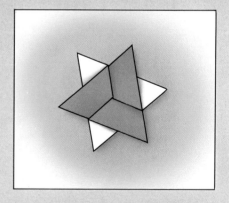

5 Interlock the flaps to hold them in place.

EIGHT-POINTED STAR

You will need:
- **thin paper**
- **scissors**
- **silver spray paint**
- **glitter**

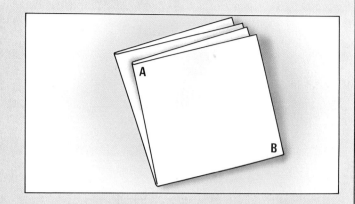

1 Cut a 20 cm square of paper and fold into four.

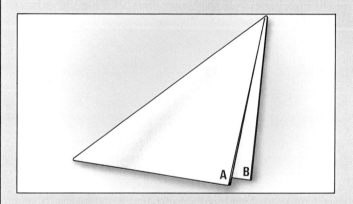

2 Fold point A over to meet point B, as shown.

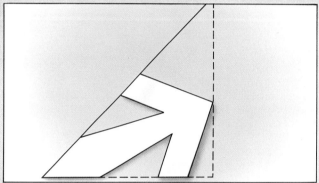

3 Cut out through all thicknesses, following the pattern shown.

4 Open out to give an eight-pointed star. Spray silver and sprinkle with glitter.

Above *Making an eight-pointed star.*

GINGERBREAD HOUSES

Part of the Christmas celebrations in Germany include the making of a gingerbread witch's house. Sometimes it is made from honey cake instead of gingerbread. It is covered with sweets and biscuits which are stuck on with icing to represent snow.

An old custom says that the house can slowly be picked apart and eaten over the twelve days of Christmas.

Right *You can use all sorts of decorations for your gingerbread house. Try using biscuits with jam-filled squares for windows, or jellied diamonds for cottage panes. Half a chocolate flake makes a good chimney.*

MAKING A HOUSE

All the ingredients can be found in any supermarket.

You will need:
- **1 packet of icing sugar**
- **egg whites**
- **3 rectangular ginger cakes**
- **a circular cake base**
- **a small palette knife**
- **a selection of small biscuits, sweets and jellied slices, chocolate buttons, cake decorations, coloured wafers and *lebkuchen*.**

1 Mix up a small quantity of royal icing. Stand two of the cakes on their long sides and stick them together with icing.

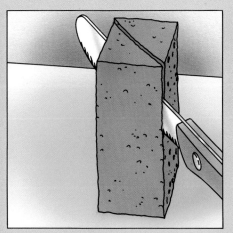

2 Use more icing to stick the cake to the base. Stand the third cake on its end and cut down the length diagonally, using a bread knife.

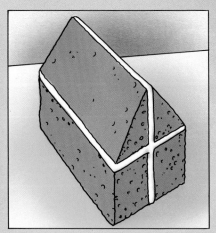

3 Use these two sections to make the roof of the house. Hold in place with icing.

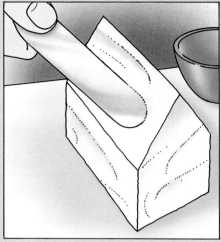

4 Mix up a bowl of stiff royal icing. Do not make too much or it will set before you can use it up and will be wasted.

5 Sort out the biscuits and sweets. Begin to stick on the decorations, working on one wall at a time. Using your palette knife, cover the wall with a thin layer of icing. Press the biscuits on while it is still soft.

6 On the front, make a door and two windows. Give them shutters and decorate the edges with tiny sweets.

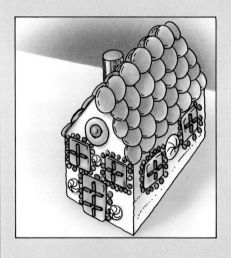

7 When the walls are set, tile the roof and make a chimney. Work from the edge of the roof up towards the ridge. Push the biscuits into the icing at an angle so that they overlap like real roofing tiles.

8 Make icicles to hang from the roof by dribbling soft icing off a spoon. Add a blob of snow to the chimney top.

9 Finally, ice the ground round the base of the house and make a path and garden using liquorice allsorts and other sweets.

FATHER CHRISTMAS PUPPETS

New toys and games often appear among the presents on Christmas morning. Puppets known as 'Jumping Jacks' or *pantins* were very popular in France in the eighteenth century. By the beginning of this century, large numbers were being produced. One German toy manufacturer called them 'Jolly Jumpers' and made them in the shape of people in national costumes, Humpty Dumpty and cats and dogs.

MAKING A PUPPET

This Father Christmas puppet is made in a similar way to these toys. It has arms and legs which move when a string is pulled at the back.

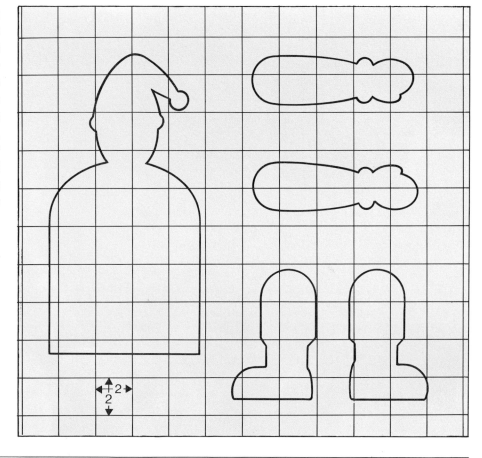

You will need:
- paper
- scissors
- white card
- coloured pens
- a knitting needle
- a darning needle
- 4 split paper fasteners
- fine cord or crochet cotton
- a curtain ring
- cotton wool
- glue

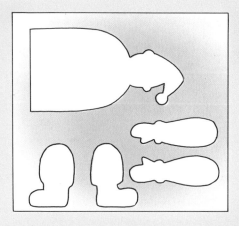

1 Scale up the drawing of Father Christmas from the pattern shown. Draw the five pieces on to paper to make a pattern.

2 Trace each part of the body on to card and cut out. Colour each section, filling in clothes and boots. Give him a beard and a red nose.

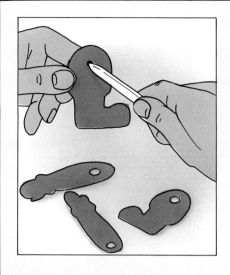

3 Using the knitting needle, make a hole near the top of each limb for the paper fastener to go through. Check that the fastener moves easily in the hole.

4 Make four more holes on the body where the limbs will join it.

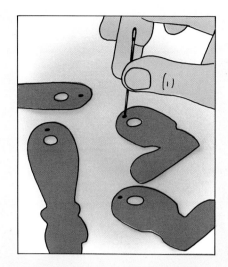

5 Make smaller holes with the darning needle for the cord to go through as shown. Do not put them too near the edge of the card.

6 Join all the parts together with fasteners. Position the limbs behind the body and take the fasteners through from the front to the back.

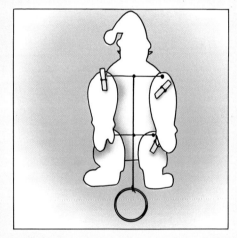

7 String the figure at the back with the limbs hanging down. Join the two arms with a thread, then the legs. Attach a third thread to the centre of the arm string, then join it to the leg string. Tie a curtain ring to the end.

8 Make a hole at the top for a hanging thread. Finally, give Santa a cotton-wool beard and snowy boots. Pull the cord to make the figure move.

ANGELS

Christmas would not be complete without a tree decorated with lights and tinsel. No one really knows when this custom began but it is thought to be a continuation of the ancient tradition of decorating the home with evergreens. These were a symbol of continuing life.

Traditionally the tree was lit by candles and topped by a Christchild angel with golden hair. Over the years the angel has been replaced by a fairy and sometimes by a Bethlehem star.

Right *Angels on the Christmas tree.*

FIR-CONE ANGEL

You will need:
- a hazel nut
- a pine cone
- glue
- gold crochet thread
- scissors
- enamel paint for features
- stiff gold paper or card
- needle and fine thread

1 Glue the hazel nut to the flat underside of the pine cone to make the angel's head. Leave to dry completely.

2 To make the hair, cut several strands of gold thread about 5 cm in length. Tie together 1 cm from one end. Glue to the top and back of the head, bringing the short ends forward to make a fringe.

3 Paint on a face using the enamel paint. Draw a pair of wings about 6 cm across on to gold card. Cut out and glue in place at the centre of the angel's back. Sew a fine thread through the hair at the top to make a loop for hanging.

CLOTHES-PEG ANGEL

You will need:
- an old-fashioned (dolly) clothes peg
- coloured pens
- compasses
- white tissue paper
- scissors
- glue
- cotton wool
- gold or silver craft foil
- tinsel

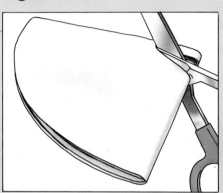

1 Using coloured pens draw a face on the head of the peg.

2 Using your compasses, draw a circle 15 cm in diameter on a double thickness of tissue paper. Cut out. Fold into four and cut across the tip to make a small hole in the centre for the peg to go through.

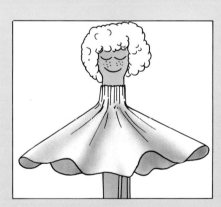

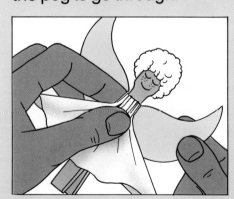

3 Attach one circle of paper at a time. Glue the edge of the centre hole to the neck of the peg, gathering all round. Add cotton wool for hair.

4 Cut out the wings from foil and glue to the back of the angel. Add a scrap of tinsel for a halo.

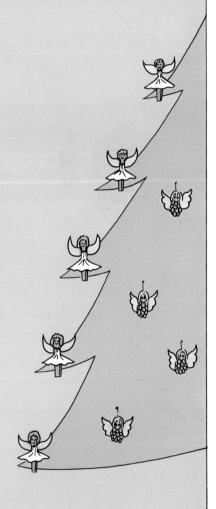

Make several angels and peg them all over the Christmas tree. A pretty alternative is to make them from different-coloured tissue or from lace doilys and to cut their wings from sequin waste.

BAKING DAY

Many years ago, one day of the week used to be set aside as baking day. As Christmas approached, many hours had to be spent in the kitchen, preparing for the festivities. There were no refrigerators and cooking was done on a range, or in an oven beside the fire. On cold winter days, children loved to crowd around the table, enjoying the heat from the big fire and waiting to taste the leftovers in the large mixing bowl. They squabbled over the 'kissing crust' taken from the freshly-baked bread and, to keep them quiet, they were sometimes given offcuts of pastry to make into shapes.

__Right__ The kitchen was often the best place to be on baking day!

CHURCH WINDOWS

You will need:
- **a baking tray**
- **foil**
- **cooking oil**
- **a rolling pin**
- **left-over scraps or a packet of shortcrust pastry**
- **a knife**
- **boiled sweets in assorted colours**
- **a small hammer**

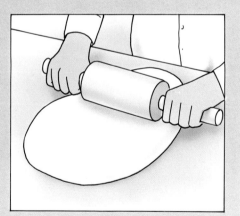

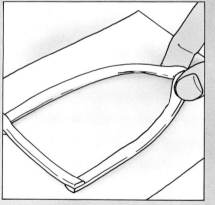

1 Line the baking tray with foil and smear with a little oil. Roll out your pastry on a floured board to a thickness of 6 mm.

2 Cut three strips 1 cm wide and lay on the foil in the shape of a church window. Wet the joins with a drop of water and press firmly together.

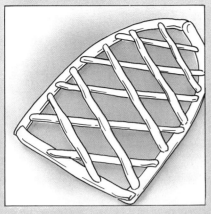
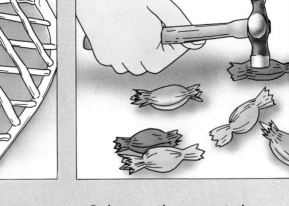

3 Cut several 6-mm strips and lay across the window frame in a diamond pattern. Moisten the underside of the top layer of strips with water and press firmly on all the joins so that the window panes will stay separate when cooking.

4 Leave the sweets in their wrappers and tap each one a few times with the hammer to break into tiny pieces.

5 Carefully pour the broken pieces into the window spaces, making a pattern of colours. Fill each space right up and press down gently with your knife.

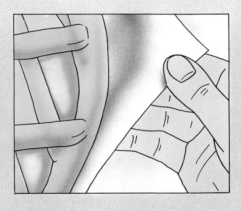

6 Bake in the centre of a warm oven (200°C; Gas 5) for about 15 minutes or until the pastry is cooked. If the oven is too hot the colours will not be bright. Always remember to use oven gloves when lifting trays in and out of a hot oven.

7 Remove from the oven and set aside until completely cool. Slowly peel the foil off the back of the window.

Look at history books to get ideas for different shaped church windows.

CHRISTMAS STOCKINGS

Many children enjoy the excitement of hanging up a stocking on Christmas Eve. Traditionally the stocking contained a rosy apple in the toe to symbolize good health and an orange in the heel for luxury. Until this century, oranges were quite rare and expensive.

There were also a few nuts, a bright new penny for wealth and a bag of chocolate coins wrapped in gold foil to commemorate St Nicholas and his generosity to the poor.

Salt was included for good luck. In the past it was very precious and often used for trading. Roman soldiers were sometimes paid in salt. Their word for salt was 'sal' and this is where the word 'salary' comes from.

Finally, the stocking contained a lump of coal wrapped in tissue as a symbol of warmth for the coming year.

You can make a stocking and fill it with small gifts for brothers, sisters or friends.

MAKING A STOCKING

You will need:
- **dressmakers' pattern paper**
- **2 pieces of quilted cotton fabric in a red and green design, or red felt, each piece 55 × 35 cm**
- **pins, needle and thread to match fabric**
- **pinking shears**
- **1 m red ribbon, 4 cm wide**
- **1 m green ribbon, 1.5 cm wide**
- **cotton wool (optional)**

1 Scale up the pattern (right) and draw out on to dressmakers' pattern paper. Cut out.

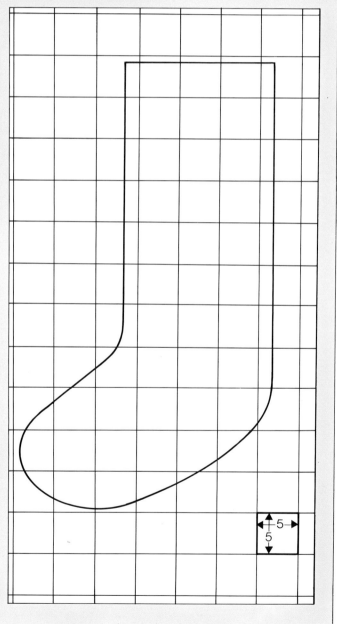

2 Pin the pattern to the first rectangle of material and cut out using pinking shears. Reverse the pattern and cut out the second stocking shape to match.

3 Turn over a 1.5 cm hem to the wrong side of each stocking top and stitch down.

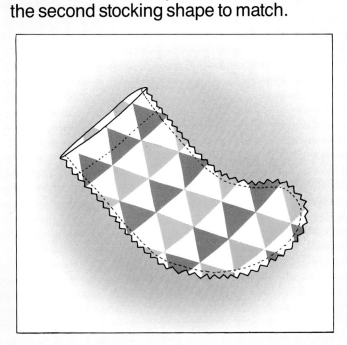

4 With wrong sides facing, pin both stocking shapes together. Stitch all round, leaving the top open. Make a loop from a strip of matching fabric 30 cm in length and stitch to the inside over the back seam.

5 Make two bows from the red and green ribbons. Sew the wide bow to the side of the stocking near the top, then add the narrow bow. Trim the ends of the ribbon If making a felt stocking, you could glue on cotton wool snow instead.

Glossary

Adobe Bricks made from clay which have been dried in the sun.

Colonies Settlements of people living in a new land. They are ruled by the country that they came from.

Fertility The ability to produce new life. People used to worship the ancient fertility gods and goddesses, so that their crops would grow.

Hindu A follower of Hinduism. This is an Indian religion but it is followed by many people throughout the world.

Lebkuchen A kind of German biscuit.

Martyred Tortured or killed for having certain beliefs. St Lucia was killed for believing in Christ.

Nordic People or things that come from Denmark, Sweden, Norway and Iceland. Also known as Scandinavian.

Norsemen Ancient Scandinavian people.

Pagan Often used in the past to describe a person or thing which was not Christian.

Saffron The orange-coloured centre parts of a crocus, used to colour and flavour food.

Symbol An object which is used to represent a different object or idea. The dove is used as a symbol of peace, for example.

Universal Something which is understood everywhere in the world.

Winter solstice The time when the sun is furthest from the equator. This creates the shortest day of the year.

Books to read

Diana Carey and Judy Large, *Festivals, Family and Food* (Hawthorn Press, 1982)

Gillian Cooke, *A Celebration of Christmas* (Queen Anne Press, 1980)

Mary Ann Green, *Festive Crafts* (Frederick Muller, 1983)

Iris Grender, *An Old-Fashioned Christmas* (Hutchinson, 1979)

Celia McInnes, *Projects for Winter* (Wayland, 1988)

Judy Ridgeway, *Festive Occasions* (OUP, 1986)

Elizabeth Walter, *A Christmas Scrapbook* (Collins, 1979)

Bright Ideas for Christmas Art and Craft (Scholastic Publications Ltd and Ward Lock Educational Co Ltd, 1984)

Picture acknowledgements

Christmas Archive 25; Elvaston Castle Working Estate Museum 26; Hutchison Library 8; Picturepoint cover (bottom); Swedish National Tourist Office 10; Topham Picture Library 28; Wayland 20; Tim Woodcock cover (top right), 4, 6, 19; ZEFA 12, 22, 24. The cover artwork is by John Yates.

Index

Advent **6**
Angels **24**

Bethlehem **8, 18, 24**

Canada **17**
Celts **4**
Chanukah **18**
Christians **4, 6**
Christmas Eve **6, 18, 28**

Farolitos **9**
Feast of Juul **4**
Fire festivals **4, 10**
France **22**

Germany **6, 12, 20, 22**

Hindu marriage rites **18**
Holland **12**

Juleneg **16**

Kalends **4**

Nativity plays **4**
New Mexico **9**
Norsemen **4, 16**

Projects
   3-D Christmas tree **15**
   Christmas stockings **28-9**
   Church windows **26-7**
   Cracker card **15**
   Eight-pointed star **19**
   Making a gingerbread house
    20-21
   Making an Advent calendar
    6-7
   Open lantern **8-9**
   Paper-bag lantern **9**

Popcorn garlands **17**
Speculaas **12-13**
Stand-up card **14**
Star Boy's hat **11**
Star of David **18**
St Lucia crown **10**
Thumbprints **5**

Romans **4, 12, 28**

Saturnalia **4**
Sicily **10**
Stars **18**
St Lucia's Day **10**
St Nicholas **28**
Sweden **6, 10**

USA **17**

Winter solstice **4**